Get Crafty

Fun, Creative Crafts for Children

Ali Coghlan

MERCIER PRESS

IRISH PUBLISHER – IRISH STORY

MERCIER PRESS
Cork
www.mercierpress.ie

© Alison Coghlan, 2016

Craftea Parties: www.craftea.ie

Ali's Blog: www.getcrafty.ie

Photography © Alan Rowlette, 2015: www.alanrowlette.ie

ISBN: 978 1 78117 378 7

10 9 8 7 6 5 4 3 2 1

A CIP record for this title is available from the British Library

A big 'Thank You' to the following shops for kindly supplying all of the gorgeous materials and props for the crafts in this book:

Avoca, Kilmacanogue, Bray, Co. Wicklow, Ireland.
Web: www.avoca.ie

Tiger Retail Ireland. Web: www.tiger-stores.ie

Art & Hobby Group, Unit 2A, Ballymount Cross Industrial Estate, Dublin 24. Email: info@artnhobby.ie Web: www.artnhobby.ie

Meadows and Byrne, The Pavilion, Royal Marine Road, Dún Laoghaire, Co. Dublin. Web: www.meadowsandbyrne.com

Printed and bound in the EU.

I would like to dedicate this book to my wonderful children, Harry and Nicole, who gladly participated in all of these fun crafts with their mum.

Contents

It's Party Time! 85

Make and Play! 123

Celebrations throughout the Year 157

Introduction

Get Crafty is a craft book for everyone. You do not have to have any previous art or craft experience to be able to enjoy the crafts.

Making arts and crafts was always part of my life growing up. As children we spent hours outside gathering flowers and leaves to make our magic potions, passed fun time on the beach collecting shells to paint, and dug into my mum's wardrobe to find something we could use to make wonderful DIY Halloween costumes. Toilet roll tubes magically turned into Christmas tree decorations and personally made birthday cards were always a treasured gift for the grannies and grandads.

However, over the years, as school, college, work and generally 'being an adult' took over, I never really got a chance to do those fun things any more; life just got in the way. It wasn't until I had my own kids a few years ago that my creativity was re-awakened and I remembered all of the fun things that my family and I had made together when I was young; in fact, no family event was ever celebrated without something handmade.

Now that I have children, it's easy to appreciate the natural creativity and vast imagination of every child and, in this diverse world where there are so many challenges, I feel it is important to harness this creativity as fully as we can. With this in mind, I started doing small arts and crafts activities with my kids and I realised just how much they enjoyed it. Yet when I talked about it with my friends, they would say to me, 'But I'm not an arty person, I wouldn't know where to start!' This inspired me to start my blog, and eventually led to me writing this book.

Get Crafty is a craft book for everyone. You do not have to have any previous art or craft experience to be able to enjoy the crafts I have included. The book gives you all the tools you need to spend quality time with your children, while creating something that will give them hours of entertainment and stimulate their imagination. Doing crafts with your kids is also a wonderful opportunity for you to switch off. Why not put away your phone, turn off the television and focus on making something special together?

Get Crafty is full of really simple things to do and make that reflect the best memories I have from my childhood. I hope it brings back some happy memories for you too, and helps you create more.

Have Fun!

Ali xx

Some Benefits of Doing Arts and Crafts with your Kids

 It teaches children to think creatively and use their imagination.

 It builds confidence and self-esteem in children.

 It helps children learn to express feelings with or without words.

 It teaches your child problem-solving skills.

 It teaches children that there are multiple ways of doing things.

 It encourages children to create their own entertainment.

 Crafts can be used as a tool to teach children numbers, colours, letters, etc.

 Most importantly: it's great fun!

Tips for Making Crafts with Children

Here are a few tips I have learned while doing crafts with my children to get you started. While I encourage the kids to help me as much as possible, remember that many of the crafts are age-dependent and will require supervision.

Time is of the essence

* Choose an appropriate time that suits both you and the child – lazy Sunday mornings or relaxed weekday afternoons work well.

* Avoid times when they are tired, busy, or there are limits on the time you have available.

* Crafts can be completed over many sessions: you can start a craft one day and finish it the next.

Be prepared

A child's attention span can be quite limited. To maximise the moment, it is a very good idea to be organised in advance.

* Get all of your 'ingredients' ready before your child sits at the table.

* Only take out what is required for each craft e.g. two 'googly eyes', not all the googly eyes! This avoids a lot of mess and saves on the clean up.

Sit together

Remember that this is quality time together. Try to avoid doing other things that might distract from the moment. Forget the washing and the cleaning. Most importantly, be present and enjoy the time you have together.

Encourage them

Kids have such wild imaginations; if they want to paint the sky yellow instead of blue, encourage them. There is no right way. If you are a bit of a perfectionist and you feel like jumping in and re-organising their efforts, stand back. Does it really matter if the arms are in place of the feet and the head is too big for the body? Just sit back and see how creative the little people can be.

The mess

Arts and crafts are messy, but there are certain things you can do to contain the mess.

For smaller crafts you can place everything on a normal kitchen tray. This helps to contain the craft in one place and also makes it easier for the child to keep everything at arm's reach.

Disposable kitchen tablecloths from the Two Euro shop (or the Poundshop) are very handy for crafts. You can re-use these many times and dispose of them when you are finished. Don't forget: the memories will last longer than the mess.

What to wear

Cheap aprons, old T-shirts or Dad's shirt backwards with rolled up sleeves work very well to keep everyone clean.

Add some sparkle

Kids love glitter. You can pretty much add glitter to any craft and kids are going to burst with excitement. Instead of giving them the full tub of glitter, unless you want to be cleaning up glitter for the next month and eating glitter sandwiches every day, my advice would be to sprinkle a little bit onto their hand or a small amount onto a plate and let them use it this way.

Safety Statement

All of the crafts in this book are to be made with the direct help and supervision of an adult. Please be aware of your child's level of capability and do not leave small items like googly eyes or buttons lying around near small children. They might be a choking hazard.

Getting Started

Before you get started, there are some very inexpensive basic items that are required. You can pick up things along the way and build up a good stash of crafty things over time. Have an arts and craft recycle bin in your kitchen and fill it with useful items such as toilet roll tubes, cereal boxes, bottle tops, empty cartons, used shampoo bottles, empty juice boxes, etc.

My top 15 craft essentials to get you started:

Pritt Stick/glue dots

Googly eyes

Pipe cleaners

Pompoms

Buttons

String/ribbon

Felt

Card

Paper plates

Paints

Paintbrushes

Glitter

Tissue paper

Wool

Disposable tablecloth

Back to Basics

This chapter is all about getting back to basics, basic crafts to get you started. These are things that I make with my children all the time and most of them are made with things we already have around the house or with one or two simple ingredients. Crafts like salt dough and papier mâché have been around for years, but they are easy to master and once you learn the method you can use your imagination and make anything you like. These eight crafts are a fantastic introduction for you and your children.

Salt Dough Snowmen

Salt dough is one of my all-time favourite crafts. It is so cheap, using only three ingredients that most homes would have handy in the kitchen cupboard. It is easy to make. Children love making it as it is similar to baking, without the eating part. It is suitable for all ages, except for younger babies who might be inclined to eat the dough. Once you have mastered salt dough, there are endless possibilities, like baby handprint or footprint keepsakes, Christmas tree decorations (using cookie cutters) or jewellery. Salt dough snowmen are the perfect Christmas decoration to sit on the mantelpiece.

What you need

Plain flour • Table salt • Water • Toothpicks • Scissors
Cup • Bowl • Spoon • Oven tray • Baking paper • Paint
Paintbrushes • Ribbon, felt and any other decorations you want

How to make it

1. Preheat the oven to 150°C (fan oven)/gas mark 2/300°F.

2. Mix 2 cups of flour and 1 cup of salt together in a bowl.

3. Gradually add 1 cup of water, mixing as you go. You don't want to add the whole cup at once, as it might make the mixture too wet. If the dough does get too wet, just add in an extra bit of flour.

4. Sprinkle some flour on your worktop.

5. Place your dough on the worktop and knead for about 3 minutes, until smooth. Once you are happy with your dough you can start to make your snowmen.

6. To make four snowmen you will need to make four large, four medium and four small balls. The kids will love rolling the dough in their hands to make the dough balls.

7. When you have all of your balls completed place one large ball on a toothpick and stand in an upright position on your workspace. Squash the ball down to flatten the base of the snowman slightly. Next add a medium ball, then a small ball for the snowman's head.

8. Cut a toothpick in half using scissors and insert one piece on opposite sides of the middle ball, sharp end out, as the snowman's arms.

9. Reduce the heat in the oven to 100°C/gas mark ¼/210°F. Place your snowmen on baking paper on an oven tray and bake. The time depends on the thickness and the size of your dough but I would normally bake for about an hour and a half and then turn the oven off and leave them overnight in the oven to dry out. You will know they are cooked when they are hard and hollow to tap.

10. Once cool, you can paint with acrylic paints and decorate your snowmen with ribbon, felt, buttons or whatever you fancy!

Crafty tips

★ You can air dry your salt dough creation over a few days as an alternative to cooking it. This works better if you want to make something that's flat, as oven cooking will always somewhat change the shape of your creation.

★ You can store salt dough in a container or zippy bag in the fridge for up to a week. Make sure your container is airtight.

★ You can add food colouring or glitter to the dough to make it more interesting and fun.

★ Always keep an eye on your dough when it's cooking. Cooking too fast will make the dough crack. You can cover it with tinfoil to help prevent this and if you are worried about this, turn down the temperature.

★ You can paint your salt dough creation with clear varnish to protect your creation.

Edible Paints

My little girl, Nicole, is two years old as I write this and, like most babies, puts everything in her mouth. She absolutely loves painting and I often put out real paints for her, but most of the time I am jumping in with a wipe when she tries to eat it. Making edible paints is a great solution to this and is far more relaxing for you and for them. No more worries, just let them paint with their fingers and lick as they go. This is also a great thing to try if your baby has never painted before. It is a good tester to see whether they will automatically put the paint into their mouths and also a very good way to know when they are ready to move on to using real paint.

What you need

Small jars or containers • Natural yoghurt
Food colouring • Spoon • Rice crackers • Paintbrush

How to make it

1. Put two or three large tablespoons of natural yoghurt into a few small jars or containers.

2. Pour a few drops of the food colouring of your choice into each jar.

3. Stir the yoghurt and food colouring together.

4. If you want to make the colours more vibrant, add more food colouring.

5. Place the rice crackers out on the table in front of your little one. You can give them a paintbrush to hold or they can use their fingers. Let them paint away.

6. Eating the crackers after they have painted them is the best part!

Crafty tips

★ You can store these edible paints in a sealed container in the fridge. Just observe the 'sell-by' date on the yoghurt packs.

★ You could also pour these paints onto a clean tray for a great sensory activity for your baby to touch, feel and eat the paint.

Homemade Mini Stamp Pads and Stamps

My kids love stamping, but stamps can be quite expensive to buy, so we make our own instead. There are many different things you can use to make your own stamps. I love trying to use items that I have found around the house/kitchen. Potatoes make great stamps; you can also use other vegetables or fruits to stamp, such as peppers, apples, oranges, carrots or celery. While potato and vegetable stamps are fantastic for babies and toddlers, foam stamps are great for older children as they allow them to be more creative in designing their stamps.

What you need

Paper for stamping

For the stamp pads

Sponges • Small plastic containers • Scissors • Acrylic paints • Glue

For the stamps

Knife • Cookie cutters • Potatoes OR Apples • Carrots • Peppers OR Foam sheets • Pencil or pen • Plastic bottle tops • Scissors • Glue

How to make the stamp pads

1. Cut your sponges into squares, smaller than the size of your containers and place inside the containers.

2. Pour two parts paint and one part glue into one of your little plastic containers and mix together.

3. Mix the sponge around in the container until it is fully immersed in the paint/glue mixture.

How to make homemade stamps

Potato stamps:

All you need is potatoes, cookie cutters and a knife. Place your cookie cutter over your potato and press firmly. You will need a knife to cut around the outside to get rid of the excess potato. Remove your cookie cutter and your stamp is ready; it is that easy!

Vegetable stamps:

We try not to waste any food in our house so tired fruit and veg can be recycled as great stamps. Look out for special offers in your supermarket or local vegetable shop. Peppers make a fantastic shape if you cut them in half, and a nice shamrock shape for St Patrick's Day. Explore the shapes that other vegetables or fruits make, such as apples, carrots, celery or oranges.

Foam stamps:

This is a great one for the slightly older children of 5–12 years. They can design their own stamps using foam sheets and old plastic bottle tops. Take a sheet of foam, place your bottle top onto it and draw round the outside of the bottle top

so that you have a circle. Next, using a sharp pencil or pen, score the shape you want on your stamp into the surface of the foam sheet, inside the circle. Make sure you lean hard on it so that the shape is well etched into the foam. When you are happy with your design, you can cut out the circle from your foam and glue it to the top of your bottle top. Don't forget if you are writing letters or numbers these need to be drawn backwards onto the foam to be in the correct position when you stamp them. Press the foam shape onto one of your paint-soaked sponges and you are ready to go.

Papier Mâché Vase

Papier mâché, which means 'chewed paper' in French, is a really easy and fun craft to do, but a word of warning – if you have never made it before, this can be a messy craft (don't be afraid of the mess). Believe me, you will be delighted with the amazing things you can create; it's such gooey fun! This is a two-day craft, but it's worth the time and effort as the results are fantastic. You will need to leave your craft to dry overnight before you can complete it the next day. This is fantastic for all ages and I find it very therapeutic to do on my own or with my children. My husband secretly loves it too, but he won't admit it …

What you need

Newspapers • Long balloon • PVA glue
Water • Bowl • Paintbrush • Paint • Scissors • Vase/pint glass

How to make it

1. Rip up pieces of newspaper into long strips.

2. Blow up your balloon.

3. Mix together one part glue and two parts water in a bowl.

4. Using your paintbrush, cover one half of the balloon completely with your glue mixture.

5. Take a single strip of newspaper and place it evenly onto the surface of the balloon. Coat it with your glue mix.

6. Continue with the other strips until you have covered three-quarters of the balloon, leaving a 3-inch/7–8-centimetre section uncovered at the top of the balloon.

7. Layer the newspaper a couple of times all the way around your balloon.

8. Leave to dry overnight in a vase or pint glass. Once dry repeat 5/6/7 again and leave to dry for an hour or two.

9. When you are happy with the thickness of your vase, pierce the balloon with a knife. Using sharp scissors, trim the top of the vase to make an even surface. Gently flatten the base of the vase by pushing up the base with your fingers to create an even, flat bottom.

10. Now your vase is ready to paint. Have fun creating your own designs.

Crafty tips

★ For the vase in the pictures I used tape to mark off the sections and to create straight lines between each colour section.

DIY Chalk

Why would anyone want to make their own chalk? Because it is so much fun! This is a great summer activity to do with your children. Get creative and explore different shapes. Cupcake or ice cube trays make great moulds or, if you are really adventurous, use a toilet roll tube to make giant chalk.

What you need

Toilet roll tubes • Baking paper • Tray • Sellotape • Scissors
Ice cube/cookie trays (optional) • Colourful washable paint
Plaster (Art & Hobby Shop or similar) • Mixing bowl • Water
Card • Spoon for mixing the plaster

How to make your moulds

1. To make the moulds, I recommend using a tray as this can be quite messy; it is a good way to contain the mess in one place.

2. Cut out pieces of baking paper, line the inside of the toilet roll tubes with them and sellotape in place. You need to have a 1-inch/2–3-centimetre overlap at the top. It is important that this is as neat as possible so that the mould has a clean surface on the inside. This will allow the mixture to sit nicely inside the mould.

3. Now cut out a square of baking paper and sellotape it over the bottom of your toilet roll tubes as a base.

4. Repeat the last step with a piece of card so that the base is strong (and sellotape the card in place also).

How to make the chalk

1. Mix one cup of plaster with three-quarters of a cup of water in a bowl.

2. Pour in the paint colour of your choice and mix well.

3. Add more paint if you want a stronger colour. Mix well until the mixture starts to get thick, at which point it is ready to go into the moulds.

4. Slowly pour or spoon your mixture into your moulds. (As well as the toilet roll tubes, I also made some fun heart shapes using cheap ice cube trays).

5. Leave to dry overnight.

6. Peel off the toilet roll holders and allow to dry out for a few hours.

7. Go outside and have great fun creating colourful masterpieces. Don't worry – if the neighbours ask, the rain will wash it away!

Crafty tips

★ Add some glitter to your chalk mixture before you pour it into the moulds to make some magical sparkly chalk.

Handprint and Footprint Painting

We love making our own cards for birthdays, Christmas, Valentine's Day and other events. It is easy to add a really personal touch by doing handprints and footprints on a piece of card. Use your imagination to turn the print into something special. Right now, Pinterest.com will give you loads of ideas for shapes or animals. Googly eyes are a great way of instantly turning prints into an animal and all you have to do then is draw the rest of the shape with a marker.

What you need

Washable paint • Card • Paper/plastic plates
Paintbrush • Markers • Baby wipes

How to make it

1. Squirt some paint onto a paper plate, just enough to cover the surface of a hand or a foot.

2. Gently place your child's hand or foot onto the plate and swirl it around so that the complete base of the hand or foot is covered in paint. Alternatively you can paint the hand or foot using a paintbrush.

3. Place the hand or foot onto a piece of card. With handprints, I find it is easier if you start with the palm of the hand and gently roll it forward onto the fingers. The same technique works well with a footprint. Press the heel first onto the card and roll the foot forward to the toes.

4. Small children's natural reaction is to scrunch their hands up so you might need to do this several times before you get a good print.

5. Take turns and let them paint your hand too.

Crafty tips

★ Have some baby wipes on hand to quickly clean off the paint once you are finished.

★ Use markers to decorate your handmade cards, writing personalised messages to complement the gorgeous prints.

★ Make some colourful handprint wrapping paper. Use a roll of plain white paper and design it with your colourful handprints for those doting grandparents.

Jelly Playdough

There are many different ways to make playdough, but this is by far my favourite one because it's unbelievably soft and smells absolutely delicious. A word of warning: while this is not harmful, I would not encourage the children to eat it.

What you need

Jelly powder sachets (orange/raspberry/blackcurrant/strawberry)
Plain flour • Salt • Water • Cooking oil • Wooden spoon • Saucepan

How to make your moulds

1. Mix together 1 cup of plain flour, 2 tablespoons of salt, 1 cup of warm water and 1 tablespoon of oil in a saucepan over a low heat.

2. Stir your mixture until it forms into a nice smooth dough.

3. Add in the jelly powder sachet of your choice and keep stirring until you are happy with the consistency.

4. Place your dough on a lightly floured surface and knead it until the dough is a nice consistency.

5. The children can play with the dough using their hands, a rolling pin and some cookie cutter shapes.

6. You can store this playdough in the fridge for two to three days.

Bubble Painting

Bubble painting is so much fun as an activity to do with the children and it costs absolutely nothing. This will certainly occupy them on a rainy afternoon. It is a messy craft so it is a good idea to cover your table with a disposable cloth and place some kitchen roll under the glasses before the bubble madness begins.

What you need

Water • Paint • Straws • Washing-up liquid
Glasses • White paper

How to make it

1. Pour a good squirt of washing-up liquid into three glasses.

2. Add a squirt of paint too.

3. Stir the mixture together using a straw.

4. Add approximately 100ml of water and stir again.

5. Give the kids a straw and ask them to blow into the straw to make loads of bubbles: so many bubbles that they spill over the top of the glasses.

6. Gently put a sheet of paper on top of the bubbles to make a pretty bubble print.

7. Do this many times with different colours to create beautiful bubble art.

Crafty tips

★ You can use many containers to make bubble art, including bowls, jugs, small glasses and bottles – it just depends on the size of the bubble print you would like to make. The larger the top of the container, the larger the print.

By the Seashore

We are lucky to live close to the sea in Co. Wicklow. Brittas Bay, a sandy beach in Wicklow, holds a special place in my heart. As children, we spent all our summers down there in our wonderful mobile home, playing tip the can, spin the bottle and just having good old-fashioned free fun. Now most weekends we take a walk on the beach in Brittas Bay with our own children, blow off the cobwebs and collect stones, shells and sticks to make our arts and crafts at home. It's great fun collecting things from outside and saving them for an afternoon inside, especially when the weather is not great.

A word of warning: I use a drill in a few of these crafts. Drills are only to be used by the adult, not the children.

Driftwood Sailboats

This is a fantastic summer craft to make with the children, and a great memory and keepsake of your holiday or day at the beach. These driftwood sailboats make a gorgeous room decoration and this craft is suitable for all ages to enjoy.

What you need

Driftwood • Old pillowcase • Marker • Scissors
Twine • Drill • Hole punch

How to make it

1. Choose a nice-shaped piece of driftwood to make your boat.

2. Lay your driftwood down on top of the pillowcase and, with a marker, draw the outline of the boat's sail.

3. Cut out the sail shape with scissors and cut in half.

4. Drill a small hole through the centre of the piece of driftwood.

5. Insert a small, straight piece of wood or a stick into the hole to make your mast. If you can't find one to fit, a chopstick will work just fine.

6. Make a hole in each corner of your left sail with a hole punch.

7. Thread twine through the holes and tie onto the mast and body of the boat.

8. Do the same with the other piece of material on the right-hand side.

Shell Necklace

Collect shells the next time you are on the beach and turn them into beautiful necklaces. You could also bring the markers to the beach on a summer's day and the children could draw on them while at the beach, then bring them home to finish them off.

What you need

Shells • Permanent Markers • Drill • Ribbon

How to make it

1. Brush all of the sand off your shell.

2. Using permanent markers, draw a design on your shell with pretty colours.

3. Once you are happy with your design you can drill a hole in the top of your shell and string some ribbon through to make a lovely necklace.

Crafty tips

★ Glue on feathers, craft diamonds, buttons or other decorations to make your shells even more gorgeous.

Nursery Rhyme Stones

There are so many wonderful ways to paint stones. You can paint them with letters or numbers or Xs and Os, draw silly faces on them or make them into fish or any other animal. We transform ours into little popular nursery rhymes. These make a gorgeous bedroom decoration for a baby's room, a fun garden accessory or a paper weight for the office.

What you need

Stones • White paint • Paintbrush • Felt-tip pens • Clear varnish

How to make it

1. Paint the stones white and leave them to dry.

2. Choose your nursery rhyme depending on how many stones you have.

3. Plan out the sentences from the rhyme and choose which stones you think will match the length of the sentences best.

4. Using felt-tip pens, draw your character and write the words of the rhyme on the stones.

5. When you are finished, varnish the stones to make them last longer.

Make a Kite

Paper kite-making is a great summertime activity. Transform those simple cards and straws into a colourful kite, go outside and watch it fly.

What you need

Straws • Card • Glue • Tissue paper • Pompoms
Clear fishing wire • Scissors • Stapler • Pen or pencil

How to make it

1. Glue one and a half straws vertically to a piece of card. We used paper straws but you can also use plastic straws.

2. Glue one straw at a right angle across the first straw at the centre point.

3. Draw the outline of a kite shape around the straws with a ruler.

4. Cut out the shape of your kite.

5. String pompoms onto clear fishing wire 1 metre long and staple the wire onto the bottom of the kite.

6. Then, using tissue paper, make some long tassels and staple them onto the kite.

7. Go outside and enjoy watching your kite fly in the wind.

Mexican Ojo de Dios

This is a beautiful traditional Mexican craft. 'Ojo de Dios' (pronounced 'oh-ho-day-Dee-os'), meaning 'God's Eyes', were traditionally made by the Huichol Indians in the Sierra Madre mountains of Mexico. The four points of the Ojo de Dios represent earth, wind, fire and water. The Ojo de Dios are made to look like an eye and are commonly given to children to watch over them and protect them. This is a fantastic craft to do with a group of children – it is easy to follow and the results are amazing.

What you need

Sticks • Wool of various colours • Scissors

How to make it

1. Find two sticks that are of a similar size, width and length.

2. Choose a wool colour to begin your design.

3. Tie the two sticks together in the middle with a piece of wool of your chosen colour to hold them together to make an 'x' shape.

4. The technique for making these is 'over and around, under and around'. Take your wool and wrap it over the first stick and then around it. Wrap the wool under the next stick and then around it. There is no need to tie the wool on: if you wrap it tightly enough it will hold the end in place.

5. Continue in this way until you can see a nice diamond shape forming on the sticks.

6. Decide when you would like to change colour and cut the wool leaving 3 inches to spare so that you have enough length to tie on the new colour. The knots and ends will be hidden when you continue to wrap the wool.

7. When you have finished, cut the wool and do a double knot on the stick.

Pirate Hat

If you are having a pirate party and want a simple, cheap craft that everyone can make, this is a sure winner. From my experience, this is also a great play-date activity that can be brought home.

What you need

Broadsheet newspaper • Stapler • Black card
Pirate stickers/white card • Glue

How to make it

1. Take two sheets (four pages) of broadsheet newspaper and fold them in half.

2. Turn the newspaper so that the open ends are facing away from you.

3. Take the right-hand corner, fold it into the centre of your shape and smooth down in place. Repeat with the left-hand corner.

4. Lift the first two bottom ends, fold them up and smooth down.

5. Flip the paper over and do the same on the other side.

6. Place the hat on top of the child's head to measure the size of the head. Remove and staple the edges in the right place for that child's size.

7. Cut out a piece of black card the same size as the front part of the hat and glue it on.

8. That's it! You can either decorate with stickers, or draw and cut out a skull and crossbones in white card or paper and glue it on.

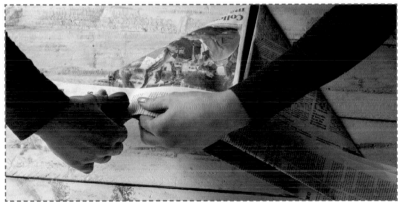

9. Your pirate hat is complete: ARGH MATEY!!!!

Ice Lolly Bracelet

This is a great example of a craft that you can make by taking something used and recycling it to make something beautiful and new. Save and collect all of your ice pop (popsicle) sticks this summer and create beautiful bracelets that everyone can wear. Be warned, this is a craft that spans a few days.

How to make it

1. Place all your ice lolly sticks in a tall glass of warm water, cover with a small plate and leave to soak overnight to soften the sticks. Large ice lolly sticks work particularly well, but you can also use the normal-sized sticks.

2. Next day, begin by gently bending each stick in your hand as you are trying to soften it up to make it more flexible. Don't worry if a few of them snap (I snap a few too); you have to be very gentle.

3. Once you think your stick is nice and bendy, curl it into a
   semi-circle shape and place inside a normal tumbler. Leave
   overnight to dry and take shape.

4. Now here's the fun part: decorate the bracelet by wrapping different-coloured twine, string or wool around it, layering it to affix the end in place.

5. To change colour, cut the first coloured twine and neatly tuck it into the twine on the back of the bracelet.

6. Continue with your new colour, until the bracelet is complete. Use a piece of tape to cover the messy ends on the inside.

7. With a knife or the top of a sharp pair of scissors, make a hole at both ends of the stick. Don't worry if it splits; this can make it easier to thread the twine through.

8. Thread a piece of twine through each end and tie a knot on the outside. Now your bracelet is ready to wear.

Sandprints

How much fun to make footprints with sand from the beach! Keep them as a memento of your holiday or beach day. Make sure you bring home enough sand for several footprints.

What you need

Sand • Old tray • Plaster (Art & Hobby Shop or similar) • Jug/bowl
Water • Spoon for mixing plaster

How to make it

1. Pour several inches of sand into your tray so that you will be able to make a print indent in it.

2. Pour a tiny drop of water into the sand to make it damp. Use your hands to mix it up a bit. This gives the sand a better consistency to be able to take a good print.

3. Make up your plaster mixture in a jug or bowl that you can easily pour from. Mix two parts plaster and one part water together. One cup of plaster is sufficient to make one big footprint or two small handprints.

4. Invite your child to place either a hand- or footprint deep down into the sand. You may need to place your hand of top of theirs to help them press down their fingers or toes to make a good print.

5. Remove their foot or hand and pour the plaster mixture slowly into the print.

6. Now leave to dry for approximately an hour.

7. Remove your print from the sand.

Crafty tips

★ Before you pour the plaster, add shells to your print to make it even more special.

It's Party Time!

A child's birthday is an exciting time for the whole family. This is a huge event for them and equally special for you. This chapter is all about easy, simple, inexpensive party ideas that make your life easier and that the children will love. Simple decoration crafts can be made together in advance of the party, and tried and tested fun party crafts for the children will keep them all busy.

Butterfly Masks

Little girls love these butterfly masks. You could cut the mask shapes in advance and then let the children do the rest; just watch how creative they can be!

What you need

White paper plates • Sellotape • Pipe cleaners • Scissors
Cake pop sticks/straws • Embellishments or stickers
Washi tape • Paper/card • Pencil/pen

How to make it

1. First make a butterfly template. Take a piece of paper or card and place your paper plate on top.

2. Then with a pencil or pen, trace around the outside of the paper plate. Put the paper plate aside. Draw out a rough shape of a butterfly onto the paper/card.

3. If you are not confident with drawing just google 'Butterfly Template' and print off a template to use. You might have to save the image to your computer and resize it using your paper plate as a guide before you print it.

4. Once you are happy with your template, place it on the paper plate and draw around the outside. Cut out the shape.

5. Next, take two pipe cleaners and twist the top of them around your finger to make curly butterfly antennae.

6. Sellotape the antennae to the back of your butterfly. Now use scissors to cut out eye holes for your mask.

7. I used cake pop sticks and stuck them together with sellotape to make one long stick to hold the mask, but a straw or any stick that is long and straight will do just fine.

8. You can wrap the stick in pretty washi tape (decorative tape) and then sellotape it onto the side of the mask.

9. Now the fun part! Decorate your masks with embellishments, craft diamonds, stickers, feathers or glitter, or just colour them with markers.

Ladybird Balloons

No party is complete without balloons, so why not make some fun ladybird balloons as a party craft and a going home gift. Children of all ages will enjoy this craft and then they can play with them outside once they are dry. If this is a party craft, paint the plates a day in advance.

What you need

Red balloons • Paper plates • Googly eyes • Black marker
Black tape or sellotape • Red & black paint
Paintbrush • Scissors • Pencil

How to make it

1. With a pencil, draw the shape of three little legs on either side of a paper plate and cut out the legs. If you need more than one ladybird, do this for as many plates as you need.

2. Paint the paper plate with red paint and leave it to dry. Then paint the legs black and leave them to dry.

3. Take a length of black tape or sellotape that is two and a half times the width of the paper plate. Fold it over to make a double-sided piece of tape, ensuring that the sticky side is on the outside. Place the tape down the centre of the plate.

4. Blow up a red balloon, tie a knot in the end and then place the balloon on its side on top of the tape.

5. There will be excess tape on the back of the plate, pull this underneath the plate and stick it in place.

6. Use a black marker to draw the ladybird's spots onto the plate and then onto the balloon.

7. Stick two googly eyes onto the balloon and draw the ladybird's face. Bend the legs on the ladybird plate so that it stands.

8. That's it: enjoy playing with the ladybirds in the garden.

Birthday Party Piñata

This is so much fun to make leading up to a birthday party and simpler than it looks! The children love getting involved in handmaking their very own DIY birthday party piñata filled with sweets, and are so proud when they get to show it off to their friends before they all bash it at the party.

What you need

Old cardboard box • Scissors • Tissue paper • Glue • Tape
Pencil • Pipe Cleaners • Ruler • String • Sweets
A firm stick (to hit the piñata with!)

How to make it

1. Take a ruler and draw out the number of your choice on the cardboard. Here I chose the number five for my son's 5th birthday. You can make this in any size; mine is 18 inches tall.

2. Cut out two identical shapes.

3. Next cut out 3-inch-wide strips of cardboard to use to cover the sides of your piñata.

4. Using the tape, assemble your piñata, matching the edges neatly. Leave a flap open and un-taped at the top of your piñata.

5. Cut 2-inch-wide strips from the coloured tissue paper and snip a fringe halfway up one side. Use as many colours as you like. A quick way to do this is to fold the tissue paper over a few times before you snip the fringe.

6. Once you have prepared all your tissue paper, start gluing the fringing onto your piñata. Alternate the colours to create the lovely piñata effect. Overlap the tissue paper so that the only part that gets shown is the fringe and the un-fringed part is the bit you glue down. You can put as many layers as you like on the piñata as long as you completely cover the cardboard.

7. Now the fun part! When you have finished covering your piñata, fill it will sweets or mini prizes for the children.

8. To secure your piñata cut two small holes in the flap at the top of the piñata that you made earlier. Then also cut two holes in the corresponding edges of the piñata. String pipe cleaners through the holes and twist together to secure your piñata.

9. Make a hole in the top of your piñata and use string to hang it.

Pink Party
Bubbles and Wands

As a little girl, I fondly remember visits to my Granny Mena's house. We all had fun together making bubbles and then playing with them in her back garden. Something that was so simple is a wonderful lasting memory for me to this day, not just because we were playing with bubbles but because she made the bubbles with us!

What you need

Garden wire • Scissors • Mixed beads
Washing-up liquid • Washable paint • Water

How to make bubble wands

1. Cut a piece of garden wire approximately 25cm in length (for a small wand) or 35cm (for a large wand).

2. Thread your colourful beads onto the top of the wire to create the top part of the wand. I used eighteen beads, but this will depend on the size of your beads.

3. Twist the top end of the wire into a circular bubble wand shape and twist the end of it in place where the shape meets the handle. Trim any excess wire that secures the head.

4. Then add the beads to the handle of the wire from the bottom up. To secure the bottom of the wand, twist the wire up the length of the bottom bead and slot the end of it into the bead's hole to hold it in place.

How to make the bubbles

1. Mix together one cup of water with one and a half tablespoons of washing-up liquid.

2. Add in one teaspoon of paint. You can use any colour of paint as long as it's washable paint.

3. Mix together thoroughly, dip your bubble wand into the mixture and get started!

Crafty tips

★ You can make the top of your wand any shape you like, for example a heart or a star.

Fringed Garlands

A fringed garland is an easy, colourful decoration that you can make for any party or special occasion. It can be made for any celebration throughout the year by theming the colours to the party event.

What you need

Coloured tissue paper • Baker's twine or ribbon
Scissors • Glue

How to make it

1. Fold two pieces of tissue paper measuring 20 x 30 inches/ 50 x 75 centimetres in half lengthways and then fold in half again the other way.

2. Face the tissue paper with the open long edge towards you.

3. Using scissors, cut strips towards the top fold leaving about 1.5 inches/4 centimetres at the top untouched.

4. Unfold the tissue paper. There will be one or two strips that you will need to manually cut as they were on the folds of the paper and will not be the same width as the others.

5. Now open and spread the strips out evenly on both sides. Cut the long opened-out piece of tissue paper in half; this will make two tassels.

6. Take the first half of the paper and open it out completely.

7. Take the end nearest to you, fold over a 1 inch/2 centimetre width and smooth out. Continue folding until you reach the end.

8. To finish, cut one strip of paper from your tassels and glue it around the top of the complete tassel to create a loophole.

9. Create twelve tassels in total using as many different colours as you like. I used three colours, creating four tassels for each colour.

10. Once you have all of your tassels completed, string a piece of baker's twine or ribbon through all of the loops and hang it as a beautiful decoration for your party.

Mess-free Dyed Pasta

Colour dyeing pasta has been around for years; it is one of those fantastic classic crafts that you will enjoy together, especially on another rainy day! This is a mess-free way of doing it, too. It's also great for helping with the development of children's fine motor skills and hand–eye coordination. This is my standby for a quick party craft or a family occasion activity, as it is suitable for all ages. For a party, it is a good idea to make the coloured pasta in advance, pour it all into the middle of the table and let the kids make pasta jewellery.

What you need

Pasta shapes • Acrylic paint • Ziplock bags • Baking paper

How to make the pasta

1. Place a handful or two of dried pasta into a ziplock bag.

2. Squirt in two tablespoons of paint in the colour of your choice.

3. Zip the bag closed and (here's the fun part!) shake it, using your hands on the outside of the bag to massage the paint into the pasta inside the bag.

4. When you think the pasta is completely covered in paint, pour it out onto a piece of baking paper.

5. Make a few different colours and leave them all to dry overnight on the baking paper.

Things to make with colourful pasta

1. Jewellery. Make necklaces and bracelets using pipe cleaners or twine.

2. Pasta art. Use your pasta to create beautiful designs on a piece of card.

3. Pasta sculptures. Get creative and try making some fun shapes like cars or trains.

Crafty tips

★ To make necklaces or bracelets, use penne or rigatoni pasta as you can thread string or pipe cleaners through them quite easily.

★ Pretty pasta shapes, such as bow-shaped pasta, are also great as you can still use them to decorate even though they don't have holes.

★ Dyed pasta and pipe cleaners in a ziplock bag make a great activity at a family dinner or in a restaurant. The children will be delighted with something to do and you will be able to eat your meal in peace (for a few minutes at least!).

★ This is a fantastic craft for a DIY children's party. Make the dyed pasta with your child in advance. The party guests can enjoy making their own jewellery at the party and take it home in their goody bags.

Tissue Pompom
Party Hats

It's so much fun to plan that special party together. Party hats are a quick pre-party craft that you can make with your child a few days before the party. This adds to the excitement. Choose your colour to match them to your party theme.

What you need

White card • Ruler • Tin lid • Pencil/felt-tip pen • Tissue paper • Scissors
Stapler • Pipe cleaners • Bakers twine/ribbon • Hole punch • Glue

How to make the hat

1. Take an A4 piece of card and, using a large circular tin lid, trace the outline of a semi-circle that fits the width of the card.

2. Use a ruler to draw the rest of the shape – it should look like a section of a clock face from nine o'clock to two o'clock.

3. Cut the shape out and fold the card into a cone shape and staple in place.

How to make the tissue pompom

1. Cut out six sheets of tissue paper, 9.5 x 8 inches/24 x 20 centimetres.

2. Taking the short side, fold accordion style, in 1 inch/2.5 centimetre-wide strips.

3. Fold the pompom in half to make a crease at the centre and secure at this crease with a pipe cleaner.

4. Use scissors to round out the corners of the tissue pompom on both ends to create a petal shape.

5. Separate the layers of tissue paper in the same direction on one side. Repeat this on the other side. Glue your tissue pompom to the side of your hat.

6. With a hole punch, make a hole on each side of the hat and string with baker's twine or ribbon.

Edible Prince and Princess Crowns

Make some edible crowns for instant party success. Children of all ages love these, for obvious reasons ... they can even take their own crown home if it lasts that long!

What you need

Paper plates • Scissors • Icing sugar
Water • Selection of sweets

How to make them

1. Fold a paper plate in half. From the centre of the folded edge, make three cuts of equal distance into the paper plate leaving a 2-inch/2.5-centrimetre gap at the outer edge.

2. Unfold the plate and make two more cuts on each side – it will be obvious where these need to be made.

3. Bend each tip of the crown upwards to create a fully shaped crown.

4. Mix together half a cup of icing sugar and a few teaspoons of water. You want to create a thick, edible glue that's not too runny.

5. Place the edible glue and the sweets on the table and let the children decorate their crowns.

6. Leave the crowns to dry so that the icing can go hard.

7. Have fun eating all the sweets off the plates.

Make and Play!

My children always amaze me with their wild imaginations. Puddles become lava, cereal boxes are rockets and pots and pans are musical instruments. No matter how generous Santa Claus is, how often have you noticed that the cardboard box and the packaging can be the main source of fun on Christmas Day? I encourage simple play by making things with empty boxes, toilet roll tubes and other recyclables that can be found in every home.

Mini Tea Party Cups

Découpage is a fun activity that takes some time. Transform those toilet roll tubes into a pretty tea party set and invite your friends over for afternoon tea.

How to make them

1. Take several toilet roll tubes. Cut one in half for the two teacups.

2. Take another and cut out pieces from the roll that measure 4 x 1 inches/10 x 2.5 centimetres to make the handles.

3. To make a teapot, use a kitchen roll tube and cut it in half. Roll up a small piece of cardboard for the spout and glue it in place.

4. Now take a pretty napkin and cut it into small pieces.

5. Mix together one part glue and two parts water in a bowl. Paint the glue mixture onto the teacups and teapot and place strips of napkin on top of the glue. Every time you place a strip of napkin on your teacup, paint some glue on top of it.

6. Continue in this way until all the teacups and teapot have been completely covered. Leave to dry overnight.

7. With a circular lid or cup as a template, draw out the saucer shapes on paper plates or light cardboard and cut out. Paint the saucers and handles pink and leave to dry.

8. Glue the handles to the cups and leave to dry.

9. The tea set is now ready for an afternoon tea party.

Mini Ice Cream Shop

Playing shop is one of the classic children's activities. This little ice cream shop can be made in less than 30 minutes and it offers endless hours of fun and entertainment for little ones.

What you need

2 cardboard boxes • Kitchen roll tubes • Sellotape • Scissors
Pretty paper/old magazines/wallpaper • White & yellow paint
Paintbrush/roller • Gluestick • Pencil

How to make it

1. Find a small box and seal it with tape to close it completely.

2. Paint the box white and leave it to dry.

3. Paint the ends of the box yellow in even widths and leave to dry.

4. Decorate four kitchen roll tubes with pretty paper, old magazines or wallpaper. When these are dry, sellotape these together so that you have two struts to hold your roof and then affix one to each side of the box.

5. Take another cardboard box, cut it in half and flatten it out.

6. Draw three semi-circles at the bottom edge of both sides of the card (as seen in the photograph) and cut these out. Decorate as with the kitchen roll tubes.

7. Attach this to the top of the kitchen roll tubes to complete your ice cream shop and leave to dry.

8. The mini ice cream shop is now complete.

Superhero Masks

Halloween is a big event in our house. We always make our own masks and costumes and the whole family gets involved. I asked my husband, Stuart, if he would make something with our son for this book and this is the fun activity they enjoyed together. Note: this will take a few days to complete.

What you need

Balloons • Newspaper • Glue • Water • Bowl • Paintbrush
Paint • Vase/pint glass • String • Scissors • Marker • Pencil

How to make them

1. Blow up a balloon. The balloon size will dictate the size of the finished mask. For an adult mask use a larger balloon.

2. Tear pieces of newspaper into strips and then cut them into smaller pieces.

3. Mix together one part glue and two parts water in a bowl. Take your paintbrush and cover one half of the balloon with the glue mixture.

4. Paste the pieces of newspaper onto the balloon evenly, coating each strip with your glue mix.

5. Cover one half of the balloon completely and leave to dry overnight in an upright position. The balloon will sit well in a vase or pint glass.

6. The next day add another layer of newspaper to your balloon and leave to dry again overnight.

7. Once your mask is completely dry and hardened, burst and peel away the balloon. You will be left with the structure of a mask. Trim the rough edges carefully.

8. Decorate the mask with the superhero of your choice. For example, to make a Spiderman mask paint the mask red and leave to dry. Using a black marker, draw the outline of the two eyes and the black web. Paint the inside of the eyes white. Once dry use a pencil to punch out two eye holes.

9. Punch another hole on each side of the mask and attach string to hold the mask in place.

137

Pencil Snake Toppers

This is a fantastic craft to get the children geared up for going back to school. You only need four things to make these pencil snake toppers and this is a really quick craft to make.

What you need

Selection of coloured pencils • Coloured pompoms • Googly eyes
Pipe cleaners • Glue

How to make them

1. Choose which colour pompoms you would like to use for each pencil.

2. Twist a pipe cleaner around the pencil so it looks like a spiral at the top of the pencil.

3. Stick your googly eyes onto the pompoms of your choice.

4. Glue your pompom googly eyes onto the top of the pipe cleaner and that's it! You now have some cool googly-eyed snake pencils.

Matchbox Fairies

Turn an old matchbox into a magical fairy house and create cute little fairies to live inside. A sure favourite for little girls.

What you need

Large matchbox • Long matches • White paint • Pink paint • Pompoms
Coloured doilies • String or ribbon • Decorative card/paper • Glue
Scissors • A selection of pretty buttons, embellishments or stickers

How to make them

1. Remove the matches from the inside drawer of the matchbox.

2. Paint all parts of the matchbox with white paint and leave to dry. Then re-paint the outside parts pink.

3. Decorate the outside of your fairy house with buttons, doilies and other embellishments of your choice.

4. Cut out a piece of decorative paper to fit inside the bottom of the box and glue it in place.

5. Make a hole in each side of the top of the outer box and thread with string or ribbon to create a necklace.

6. To make the fairies, cut two fairy wings out of doilies and glue to the back of a matchstick with the head removed. Attach a small pompom to make the head.

7. Place the fairies inside their matchbox house, and they are ready to play with.

Milk Carton Doll's House

You don't need to go and spend a small fortune to make arts and crafts. Recycle a used milk carton into a doll's house using these few simple steps.

What you need

A large milk carton • Paper straws • Pretty paper/old wallpaper scraps
Glue • Paint • Paintbrush • Scraps of cardboard • Felt • Scissors

How to make it

1. Rinse your empty milk carton with warm water and washing-up liquid to remove any milk residue. Leave to dry.

2. Turn the milk carton to the side so the opening of the carton resembles a chimney on a house.

3. Now cut out the front panel of the carton and cut this panel into two pieces.

4. Paint your milk carton/house in the colour of your choice. Leave to dry.

5. Glue pretty paper onto the inside walls of the house.

6. Apply glue to the inside walls halfway through the house and insert one piece of the front panel to divide it into two storeys. Allow to dry.

7. Use some paper straws to make furniture for the house – a bed, table or chair. To do this, cut out small pieces of leftover card to resemble a table or a bed and cover these with coloured felt. Then cut the straws to make the legs and glue them directly onto the card. You can get as creative as you like with the outside of the house also, adding windows if you like.

8. That's it, your doll's house is finished.

147

148

Painting Marshmallow People

Never be without a bag of white marshmallows in the cupboard for the next rainy day. These are really simple but the children will have great fun making them to play with and then drop into their hot chocolate to enjoy.

What you need

White marshmallows • Toothpicks
Food colouring (red, yellow, green, blue and black)

How to make them

1. Pour a small amount of each food colouring into the lid of the bottle or into little bowls.

2. Dip the tip of a toothpick into the food colouring and draw directly onto the marshmallow.

3. Design as many funny faces as you like with loads of different colours, different shapes and coloured hair.

4. Have fun playing with your mini mallow people and when you are finished you can gobble them all up!

Crafty tips

★ The food colouring tends to spread quickly on the marshmallow so you only need the tiniest bit of food colouring on each toothpick.

Dolly Puppets

Transform some old toilet roll tubes into gorgeous dolly puppets. You can make as many as you like and put on a fun puppet show for all the family.

What you need

Toilet roll tubes • White paint • Paintbrush • Googly eyes • Markers
Coloured wool • Lolly sticks • Super glue • Ribbon • Scissors

How to make them

1. Begin by super gluing a lolly stick to the bottom inside of each toilet roll tube and leave to dry.

2. Paint your toilet roll tubes and lolly sticks white and leave to dry.

3. To make the hair, wrap the wool about fifteen times around another toilet roll tube. Slide it off the tube and, holding it firmly at the top, cut the hair at the bottom. Trim to the length you want for your dolly.

4. Glue the hair to the top of the dolly's head.

5. Stick on two googly eyes and draw on other facial features with your markers.

6. Use markers to draw on the dolly's clothes and decorate with ribbon or any other stickers you like.

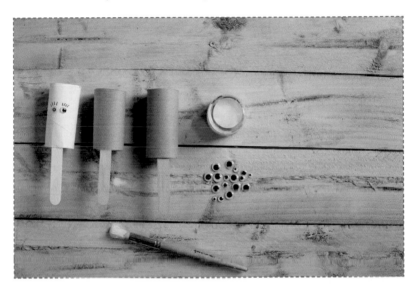

Celebrations throughout the Year

Here is a selection of holiday-inspired crafts for some of my favourite celebrations throughout the year. The Christmas period, Valentine's Day, Paddy's Day, Mother's Day, Easter and Halloween are all special times of the year, and what better way to celebrate them than by making crafts?

Homemade New Year's Eve Poppers

Make some easy DIY poppers to celebrate New Year's Eve with your family in style.

What you need

Toilet roll tubes • Tissue paper • Ribbon • Glitter card
Glue • Gold fringed party curtain (available in party shops)
Circle punch (optional) • Scissors

How to make them

1. For each popper, cut one toilet roll tube in half.

2. Place the toilet roll pieces on top of five layers of tissue paper, 15 x 12 inches/38 x 30 centimetres wide.

3. Cut up strips of coloured tissue paper and pieces of party curtain and place inside the toilet roll.

4. Roll the toilet roll up in the tissue paper leaving a tiny gap in between the two pieces.

5. Carefully tie each end of the tissue, next to the toilet roll tube, with a ribbon and make a pretty bow.

6. Decorate your poppers with glitter card. You can cut out the year or use a circle punch to make sparkly circles, for instance, then glue these on.

7. Have fun celebrating with your poppers!

Valentine's Day Rose Head Garland

It's so easy to make a rose flower. You can use paper, card, tissue or felt. Follow the steps below to make a gorgeous floral head garland.

What you need

Pink, red & green felt • Pipe cleaners • Scissors
Saucer/tin lid • Glue • Pencil

How to make it

1. Find two pipe cleaners and twist them together so that they are intertwined. Repeat this with another two pipe cleaners. Twist the two together at both ends to form the base.

2. Trace the outline of a small saucer or small tin lid onto a piece of pink felt and cut it out.

3. Cut the felt into a spiral and then roll it tightly into a rose shape. Glue the bottom of the rose to hold it in place.

4. Cut out several leaf shapes using green felt and glue these to the side of the rose. Now gently loosen out your rose and glue the bottom of the rose onto the base.

5. Make a number of roses in different colours and glue them to the base to make a gorgeous garland.

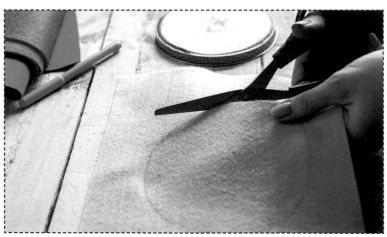

Mother's Day Pompom Bouquet

Pompom making is highly addictive. Make a gorgeous pompom bouquet this Mother's Day as a pretty alternative to flowers!

What you need

Coloured wool • Scissors • Pipe cleaners • Ribbon

How to make it

1. Take a spool of wool and wrap it around your index and middle fingers approximately eighty times. Separate your two fingers slightly when doing so and don't wrap the wool too tightly as you will need to remove it.

2. Get a small length of wool and tie it very tightly around the centre of the wool through your fingers.

3. Remove the wool from your fingers and snip the ends on both sides.

4. Fluff up your pompom with your fingers. Use scissors to give your pompom a haircut all over.

5. Take a pipe cleaner and insert it into the pompom.

6. Make several pompoms in different colours and tie them with pretty ribbons to make a perfect Mother's Day gift.

St Patrick's Day Hat

It's great fun to wear your own handmade hat to the parade or a party on St Patrick's Day.

What you need

Toilet roll tube • Orange & black felt • Elastic headband • Green paint
Green pipe cleaner • Green card • Green buttons • Scissors • Hole punch

How to make it

1. Cut a toilet roll tube in half and paint one half green on the outside. Leave to dry.

2. Decorate the rim of the hat with black and orange felt to look like a buckle.

3. Wrap a pipe cleaner around your three longest fingers to make a shamrock shape and stick a button to the middle of it. Insert this into the side of the black felt rim and glue in place.

4. Cut a circle of green card the same size as the circumference of the toilet roll and glue it on to the top of the roll.

5. Make a hole on each side of the hat with a hole punch, insert one end of the elastic headband through each hole and knot so it will stay in place.

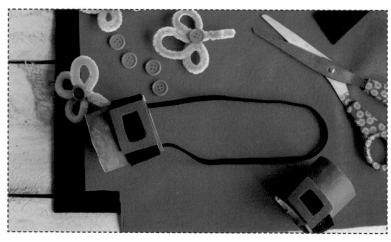

Easter Bunny Hat

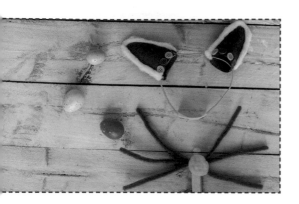

Celebrate Easter by making some easy Easter Bunny hats. The whole family will enjoy this quick craft.

What you need

2 toilet roll tubes • Pink paint • Paintbrush • Scissors
Elastic • Buttons • Cotton wool • Glue • Stapler • Lollipop sticks
White felt • Pipe cleaners • Pompoms • Hole punch

How to make it

1. Start by making the bunny ears. Take two empty toilet rolls and cut them into the shape of bunny ears.

2. Paint the bunny ears pink and leave to dry.

3. Glue the pointed ends of the ears together and decorate them with cotton wool and buttons.

4. Punch holes in each side of the ears and thread through the elastic. Cut out a small square of white felt and staple each end of the elastic to it on either side. The felt makes it soft on the child's chin.

5. To make the bunny face, twist three pipe cleaners together in the centre and glue to the top of a lollipop stick. Glue a pompom to the centre.

6. Now you are ready to hop around the garden like an Easter Bunny!

Halloween Spiders

Make some scary spooky spiders to decorate the house at Halloween.

How to make them

1. Take four pipe cleaners and twist them together in the centre.

2. Spread out the legs and bend each pipe cleaner an inch from the base to make the feet.

3. Stick two googly eyes onto two pompoms and stick them onto the spiders' legs. Stick a large pompom onto the back of the spider to create the body.

Crafty tips

★ Add a piece of string to hang them and make your spiders come alive!

Christmas Advent Calendar

Every year the build-up to Christmas Day is very exciting, especially with little people around. Why not make your own Christmas Advent Calendar to count down the days until 25 December? Have fun opening up the treats every day of the month!

What you need

13 toilet roll tubes • White paint • Paintbrush • Coloured card
Ribbon • Circle punch • Scalloped circle punch • Felt-tip pen • Glue
Sellotape • Sweets or other treats

How to make them

1. Paint the 13 toilet rolls white and leave to dry.

2. Cut each toilet roll in half and arrange 25 halves in the shape of a Christmas tree on a piece of card. Glue them in place, then cut around the outside of the card.

3. Cut out 25 circles using a circle punch. Cut another 25 smaller circles using the scalloped circle punch. Write the numbers 1 to 25 on the scalloped circles and stick them on to the larger circles so that they resemble lids.

4. Sellotape all of the finished lids to the front of each roll using a small strip of sellotape as a hinge.

5. Place a small treat inside each day. Punch a small hole in the top of the Christmas tree and thread with ribbon to hang.

Christmas Snowflakes

These snowflakes are a gorgeous Christmas decoration to instantly brighten a classroom, bedroom or garden. You can make these in any size as long as your piece of card is square in shape. Watch them twirl in the wind. Spray them with glitter spray for that extra sparkle.

What you need

Card in different colours – each snowflake needs six pieces of card

Pritt Stick • String • Scissors

How to make it

1. Fold an A4 piece of card to make a right-angled triangle. Cut off the excess card.

2. Fold the triangle in half to make a smaller triangle.

3. Turn the triangle so that the open folded edge is facing you. Begin making cuts into this side of the triangle, not the side that has a closed edge.

4. Make four or five cuts, leaving a 2-centimetre gap at the upper edge of each cut. Repeat this for each of the other five pieces of card.

5. When you have six completed triangles you can begin to assemble them.

6. Open a triangle out fully. Take the two centre flaps and fold them over onto each other and glue in place. Flip your craft over to the other side and glue the next two flaps together. Repeat this step until all flaps have been glued and you are left with one completed piece of the snowflake.

7. When you have six finished pieces, glue them to each other at their bases to make a completed snowflake.

8. Punch a small hole in the top of the snowflake and thread with string to hang.

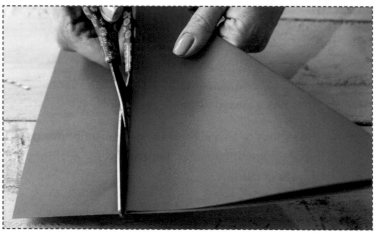

Acknowledgements

To my husband, Stuart, my number one supporter, you really are a saint to put up with me and my craft mess. Thanks for helping me for weeks on end with making the crafts every night and for encouraging me, loving me and being there for me every step of the way.

To my beautiful children, Harry and Nicole, this book would never have happened if it wasn't for you two rascals. Thank you both for opening my eyes to the world again in a different way, I love you both so much.

I would like to thank my mum, Miriam, for being the best mum I could ever ask for. It is only now I have my own children that I fully appreciate everything you ever did for me. Thank you for the hours of babysitting and delicious dinners while I was making this book. It would never have been completed without your endless support.

Thank you to Jim, for always being there with the best advice for Stuart and me.

Thanks to Suzanne for all your help and support over the years.

For giving me that extra push when I needed it most, a big thank you to Jilly Clarkin, Sinead De Brun, Victoria Redford and Ciara Moore.

Thank you also to the following for their help throughout this project: Robert Lowe, Rachael Murphy, Audrey Hamilton, Laura Steerman and Sharyn Coghlan.

Thank you so much to my Auntie Carol for all your editing work; it was so generous of you and I appreciate it so much.

Keelin, Erin, Jacob, Luke and Hugo, the gorgeous children of my friends, thank you all for coming to the party and agreeing to being photographed.

Thank you to Alan Rowlette for all the beautiful photographs for the book. It was a pleasure working with you and getting to know your family.

Thank you to Dominic Perrem for making all of this happen. You believed in me and this book from the outset. It's been lovely getting to know you.

And finally to my grandmother, Mena, the most positive person in this world, I want to be just like you when I grow up.